BEYOND THE POLE

The radio scripts

by Neil Warhurst and Paul Barnhill

‖‖ SAMUEL FRENCH ‖‖

samuelfrench.co.uk

FOR AMATEUR PRODUCTION ENQUIRIES

UNITED KINGDOM AND WORLD
EXCLUDING NORTH AMERICA
plays@samuelfrench.co.uk
020 7255 4302/01

Each title is subject to availability from Samuel French,
depending upon country of performance.

THINKING ABOUT PERFORMING A SHOW?

There are thousands of plays and musicals available to perform from Samuel French right now, and applying for a licence is easier and more affordable than you might think

From classic plays to brand new musicals, from monologues to epic dramas, there are shows for everyone.

Plays and musicals are protected by copyright law so if you want to perform them, the first thing you'll need is a licence. This simple process helps support the playwright by ensuring they get paid for their work, and means that you'll have the documents you need to stage the show in public.

Not all our shows are available to perform all the time, so it's important to check and apply for a licence before you start rehearsals or commit to doing the show.

LEARN MORE & FIND THOUSANDS OF SHOWS

Browse our full range of plays and musicals and find out more about how to license a show
www.samuelfrench.co.uk/perform

Talk to the friendly experts in our Licensing team for advice on choosing a show, and help with licensing
plays@samuelfrench.co.uk   020 7387 9373

Acting Editions

BORN TO PERFORM

Playscripts designed from the ground up to work the way you do in rehearsal, performance and study

---

Larger, clearer text for easier reading

Wider margins for notes

Performance features such as character and props lists, sound and lighting cues, and more

---

+ CHOOSE A SIZE AND STYLE TO SUIT YOU

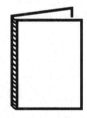

STANDARD EDITION

Our regular paperback book at our regular size

SPIRAL-BOUND EDITION

The same size as the Standard Edition, but with a sturdy, easy-to-fold, easy-to-hold spiral-bound spine

LARGE EDITION

A4 size and spiral bound, with larger text and a blank page for notes opposite every page of text. Perfect for technical and directing use

---

LEARN MORE | **samuelfrench.co.uk/actingeditions**

MUSIC USE NOTE

USE OF COPYRIGHT MUSIC

ABOUT THE AUTHORS

Neil Warhurst and Paul Barnhill

The radio series *Beyond the Pole* was the first collaboration between writer/actors Paul Barnhill and Neil Warhurst. They have gone on to script and perform in many BBC comedy series, including *Edge Falls* (starring Sarah Lancashire and Mark Benton), *The Spaceship* (starring James Fleet) and *Clayton Grange* (starring Anthony Head). Neil later adapted Beyond the Pole into the feature film of the same name. Paul is now Artistic Director of Goofus Theatre, and has recently staged productions of two of Neil's plays: *Taking Charlie* and *Dumbheads*.

As actors, Neil and Paul have worked for over twenty-five years in theatre, film and television. At the time of publication they are writing and performing *Space Junk*, a TV comedy series based on their cult radio sci-fi: *The Spaceship*.

BEYOND THE POLE - EPISODES 1-6.

First broadcast on Wednesdays from 26th May 2000, 11.15pm, on BBC Radio 4. The cast was as follows:

Narrator	Sam West
Brian	Paul Barnhill
Mark	Neil Warhurst
Graham	Kim Wall
Interviewer	Adjoa Andoh
Sandra	Becky Hindley
Terje	Ben Crowe
Ketil	Harry Myers

By Paul Barnhill and Neil Warhurst

Adapted by Neil Warhurst into the film, *Beyond the Pole*, produced by Shooting Pictures, and released in 2010, starring Stephen Mangan, Rhys Thomas, Mark Benton, Rosie Cavaliero and Alexander Skarsgard.

EPISODE ONE

Scene One

NARRATOR The Arctic. Barren, windy, packed with snow, and cold. Very cold. A vast wilderness of ice sheets and freezing ocean, just asking to be conquered, but which few are brave enough to take on.

Scene Two

BRIAN's *kitchen: Int.*

Effects spitting, frying fat.

BRIAN Danger's always thrilled me. I remember my grandad pushing me around as a toddler. I'd sit there, on the lawn mower, my legs dangling near the blades as they sliced through the green stalks. It was super...

INT Does not the tragedy of what happened to your father put you off a little?

BRIAN Not really. My dad would always encourage us to try new things, feel and touch new experiences. He misjudged that particular mountain and unfortunately that was the end of him, but I know he's with me and would encourage me to follow my destiny...

Scene Three

The gym: Int.

Effects thud of feet, hum of running machine (under).

MARK *(out of breath)* Why do I do it? That's like asking, why does someone eat a biscuit?

INT Biscuits are nice. You'll be walking for three months in temperatures fifty below zero...?

MARK Why do people do anything? Because they want to. If there's a biscuit on a plate, you eat it. It's the same with the North Pole. It's there and I want it.

Scene Four

NARRATOR Brian Tongue and Mark Bark-Jones are two men. Their aim? To walk across the most inhospitable terrain on Earth, to the North Pole.

Fade out.

NARRATOR Episode One. "Why?"

Scene Five

Reading room: Int.

Effects pages being turned, the odd cough.

MARK *(whispering)* We're here in the reading room of the Royal Geographical Society. All the explorers come here... to plan their routes.

Effects map being flattened out.

This place is full of history. It's very exciting.

INT Do you have any particular heroes?

BRIAN Yes. For me it has to be Bill Oddie. I've always been interested in bird watching and I love a good laugh, which is what this whole Pole attempt is about. That chuckle of his used to send me into hysterics. Britain at its best, nature-loving and a laugh!

MARK Keep your voice down, Brian.

INT There's nobody in here.

MARK That's not the point.

INT Tell me about your British record attempt?

BRIAN Well, we're hoping to walk the six hundred miles from the edge of Siberia to the Pole. Unsupported.

MARK Which means we're allowed no contact or assistance from land or air.

INT Hasn't that been done before?

BRIAN Well spotted. While we were in the planning stage two guys, Steve Martin and Dave Mitchell, beat us to it. Walked it in ninety-two days.

INT So where does that leave your record attempt?

MARK Well, we're going to do it quicker.

BRIAN Ninety-one days.

MARK Even ninety. Who knows? Might do it in a week.

Laughter.

INT Would you like to join the ranks of great adventurers?

BRIAN No, we're not going to the Pole to suffer. We're going to have a good time—

MARK Immortality would be a bonus.

BRIAN Oh, come on—

MARK No, no, we're part of a long heritage of English explorers, following in the footsteps of Livingstone, so to speak...

BRIAN Yea, well, Livingstone was Scottish.

Pause.

Peary was American. Columbus was Portuguese. Amundsen was Norwegian.

MARK Right.

BRIAN Try Scott. He was an Englishman. Died though, unfortunately. Froze to death in the Antarctic. *(Laughing)* That's a cheery thought, eh?

MARK Keep the noise down. Brian...

Scene Six

NARRATOR We followed Brian and Mark through to their journey's end. As they prepare for departure, our explorers cannot possibly predict where that "end" will be, or what form it will take. It is a critical time.

Scene Seven

Storeroom: Int.

Effects footsteps. Door opening.

BRIAN ...and in here, is all the equipment!

INT *(slight laugh)* Wow!

MARK Yes, I know. Looks a great deal. But all absolutely vital.

BRIAN Except for Sandra over there. That's my wife.

SANDRA Hi.

BRIAN She won't be coming. Just helping us pack.

SANDRA Lucky me.

BRIAN Is your lass coming over, Mark?

MARK No, she's a bit busy...

INT That's Melissa, your wife?

MARK Yes, my rock, my foundation. I hate to leave her in London for another cold winter—

INT She's a writer, isn't she?

MARK Umm. It breaks my heart to leave—

INT What sort of books does she write?

MARK Fantasy. Fantasy literature.

INT *(laughing)* I wondered what you'd call them.

BRIAN *and* **SANDRA** *snigger.*

MARK Um, over here is the general gear, ranging from skis to sleeping bags, rucksacks to MSR cooker—

Effects clatter of items lifted.

HF radio—

BRIAN PRB beacon—

MARK *(showing off)* Rope, Swiss army knife—

BRIAN *(competitively)* Ski sticks, skins—

MARK Snow shovel, ice axe—

BRIAN Windsail, paracord—

MARK Shot gun—

SANDRA First-aid kit.

Slight pause.

MARK All the gear will be strapped onto these two six-foot sledges—

SANDRA I'm making sure they've plenty of Caneston Powder for crutch rot.

BRIAN Yes, my love—

SANDRA And Lomotil for diarrhoea. Drugs, painkillers, cream for cracking hands, plasters for blisters and antiseptic for wounds.

BRIAN Good.

SANDRA And haemorrhoid cream for Mark.

MARK Thank you, Sandra. In all, we'll each be pulling a weight coming in about three hundred and ninety-four pounds—

SANDRA Brian?

BRIAN Yes, my love?

SANDRA What are these doing in here?

BRIAN I don't know...

SANDRA *(quietly)* Liar.

BRIAN Sandra, I've really no idea.

Effects door bursting open.

GRAHAM Yo, guys! How's it going?

BRIAN Good, Graham. Great.

GRAHAM What's the matter with her face?

MARK This is Graham. He'll be manning the radio base back in the UK.

GRAHAM Yea, just popping out for some chips. Want anything?

BRIAN Aye, get me a double sausage. Oh, d'you know how these got in here?

GRAHAM Rubber johnnies...? You dirty buggers! You been hearing about those Eskimo customs? Nice one—

Effects door slam.

SANDRA What are you planning to do out there?

BRIAN Sandra, I've no idea what he's on about...

Scene Eight

NARRATOR The days leading up to departure are indeed tense and frenetic. The whole, complex operation must be checked and double checked. Brian and Mark must also ensure they are physically prepared for the harsh Arctic climate.

Scene Nine

The deep freeze: Int.

Effects hum of freezer.

BRIAN *(shivering)* This was Mark's idea. We should be out there in the restaurant having a curry, not sat in their deep freeze.

MARK Brian has a more relaxed approach to training.

BRIAN As long as I've a good breakfast inside me, and my dad's lucky boots on me feet, I'm up for anything.

INT *(freezing)* So, are you both good friends?

BRIAN We have to be. On the ice, there's got to be one hundred per cent trust, eh Mark?

MARK Yea. We met as students at Loughborough Uni—

BRIAN —in the Outdoor Pursuits Society—

MARK There's a funny story to that actually—

BRIAN Yes. Very funny. Tell her Mark...

MARK There was this climbing expedition to the Cheddar Gorge. And it was funny because I'm very partial to cheese—

BRIAN Not that story—

MARK But poor Brian's allergic to dairy products—

BRIAN No Mark, the climbing story.

Pause.

I was climbing up this hundred foot, overhanging drop. I knew what I was doing. It was going smoothly. Meanwhile, Mark was absailing down the same face—

MARK I knew what I was doing. It was going smoothly.

BRIAN But Mark landed on my shoulders—

MARK Brian's cord got tangled in mine—

BRIAN And we were stuck, halfway up a cliff—

MARK We must have been hanging there for, what? Hour? Couple of hours?

BRIAN That's right.

MARK And we got on very well. In fact, we really got to know each other. That's where we found out, for instance, I liked cheese, and Brian was allergic.

BRIAN Once you've been hanging from a cliff face, nose to nose for hours, you know that's the sort of guy you could be in a tent with for ninety days.

MARK Yea. *(He laughs)* And still have a good time! I suppose we enjoy, "hanging around together", eh Brian?

Pause.

INT *(shivering)* Sorry, I'm a bit chilly, I'll have to go out—

BRIAN Yea, I think I'll join you...

Scene Ten

The airport: Int.

Effects hum of voices. TANNOY.

TANNOY EasyJet Flight MA434 to Malaga is now boarding at Gate Seven...

NARRATOR *(voiceover)* Tuesday, February fourteenth. The day of departure has arrived. As the flight leaves Gatwick in thirty minutes, Brian is making his final goodbyes to Sandra. Melissa, meanwhile, has failed to turn up...

BRIAN Give us a smile, love.

SANDRA *(hushed)* So you're not going to meet anybody out there?

BRIAN *(also hushed)* No—

SANDRA No playing away from home?

BRIAN Course not. We took them out of the box, didn't we...

MARK *(interrupting)* What's the time now?

BRIAN Time we went.

MARK Umm.

BRIAN Never mind, Mark. You know what she's like.

MARK What is she like? I've forgotten.

GRAHAM *(approaching)* Right boys, you couldn't if you get the chance, bring back a few packs of cigs?

MARK From the Pole?

GRAHAM No, you know, from Duty Free.

BRIAN Yea, we'll sort you out.

GRAHAM Cheers, lads.

SANDRA *and* BRIAN *begin kissing.*

SANDRA I love you, Brian.

BRIAN I love you too.

They embrace warmly.

MARK I love you.

BRIAN What?

MARK Um. I love you too... Sandra. Tell Melissa, er, just tell her goodbye.

SANDRA I will. Bye Mark.

MARK *(going)* Yea...

GRAHAM Look out for those Eskimos, Brian!

BRIAN *(distant)* Yea, bye...

Pause.

SANDRA What's all this with Eskimos?

GRAHAM Oh, that's funny, right...they say, if an Eskimo man makes a new friend, it's tradition to ask this new friend to share the Eskimo wife. It's a common courtesy apparently.

SANDRA Oh.

GRAHAM It's probably bollocks love. Let's get you home.

Scene Eleven

NARRATOR Even before their unsupported trek can begin, Brian and Mark have to fly the two thousand miles from Gatwick, via Moscow, to Arkhangel, and then by DC6 to Novaya Zemlya in Siberia. Their final destination? Sredny, an old Soviet military base on the edge of the Arctic – a journey which, in itself, would prove hardship enough for most everyday folk.

Fade.

Scene Twelve

Snowy field: Ext.

Effects wind. Distant barking of a dog.

INT So this is it. How does it feel?

BRIAN Smashing. Great. This is where it all begins.

MARK *(groaning)* Bloody awful.

BRIAN Come on, Mark. Put your cagoule on.

Effects rustling of jacket.

MARK I feel like shit.

BRIAN It was a long journey.

INT Mark's not too good at flying?

BRIAN No, no. He's an experienced flyer, just not too good with the duty free bar. Still, at least we've made it this far.

INT Shame the equipment hasn't.

BRIAN Yea, that's unlucky. Bit of a mix up in the transfer at Arkhangel.

Effects trickle of urine against wood.

BRIAN Still, it's not so bad, they're doing their best to trace it. See that hut over there with the smoke coming out the top? The lovely Svetlana's in there, rustling up something for our dinner. And I might follow Mark's example—

Effects urine trickles to a halt.

MARK Brian...

BRIAN —and indulge in a little oral refreshment.

MARK Brian. I can't do my flies up.

BRIAN Why not?

MARK My fingers are too cold.

BRIAN Come here. Let's have a go.

Effects **BRIAN** *struggling with* **MARK***'s zip.*

BRIAN All that training, eh Mark? There we are. You want to get a loop of string around it. So you can do your business without taking your mitts off...

Scene Thirteen

NARRATOR Instead of asking "why?", perhaps we should be asking "when?", or even "if?" The wrong equipment is one thing, but no equipment is entirely another matter.

Scene Fourteen

Russian pub: Int.

Effects glasses clattering. Low Russian voices.

INT Are there any lessons to be learnt?

MARK Don't let Sandra write out baggage labels.

BRIAN You're blaming Sandra?

MARK I'm not blaming her, I'm just saying she's got very poor handwriting.

BRIAN Leave her out of it...

Scene Fifteen

NARRATOR Once out in the unforgiving Arctic, Brian and Mark can blame no one but themselves, and there will be no more room for error. They must trust only in each other, for each other, is all they will have.

Scene Sixteen

Russian pub: Int.

Effects louder pub sounds. Russian singing.

MARK Never trust a woman, Brian.

BRIAN I can't believe you're giving me advice about women. You couldn't even get your lass to see you off at the airport!

MARK She's very busy!

BRIAN What, researching her porn! What does that involve, eh, Mark?

MARK Watch it, spotty!

BRIAN Don't start Mark.

MARK Spotty, greaseball.

BRIAN You're pathetic.

MARK One little pack of condoms and your whole relationship goes array.

BRIAN What did you say?

Pause.

Why mention the condoms again, Mark? It was you! You planted them in the medical box!

MARK What are you talking about?

BRIAN You little shit!

MARK Look...it was just a joke...

BRIAN Do you know how much trouble you've caused?

MARK I was jealous, OK? You're so together, so bonded, so luvy, so close—

BRIAN *(shouting)* Yea, not any more!

Effects pub noises subside.

Effects chair scrape as **BRIAN** *stands.*

Come on. Let's have this one outside. Now!

Effects the pub goes quiet.

MARK *(quietly)* Listen Brian, you're tired, you're a little drunk. Let's talk about this—

BRIAN Outside!

Pause.

INT Would you like me to switch off the microphone?

MARK Umm. Yes.

Effects tape switched off.

Shostokovich, Symphony No 10 (under).

NARRATOR Next week on *Beyond The Pole*...

Scene Seventeen

The tent: Int.

Effects wind buffeting canvas.

BRIAN/MARK *(singing)*

NORBURTON'S SUET, THE SUET FOR THE LADS, IT GIVES YOU A GLOW, WHEN YOU'RE IN THE SNOW AND WHEN YOU'RE FEELING SAD...

Scene Eighteen

Russian pub: Int.

Effects pub sounds.

INT We spoke to Zola, a worker in one of your grandfather's factories—

MARK My grandfather gave employment to—

INT She was twelve. She was making those little gloves that stretch to fit all hand sizes.

Scene Nineteen

On the ice: Ext.

Effects gale blowing.

MARK *(shouting)* This is the last time I go exploring with someone who's got a circumcised penis!

Cut out.

End of episode

EPISODE TWO

Scene One

NARRATOR Last week on *Beyond The Pole*...

Reading room. Int.

BRIAN We're walking six hundred miles across the ice, unsupported, to the North Pole.

INT Hasn't that been done before?

MARK Yes, but we're going to do it quicker.

Scene Two

A Snowy field: Ext.

Effects wind.

MARK Brian. I can't do my flies up.

BRIAN Why not?

MARK My fingers are too cold.

Scene Three

Russian pub: Int.

BRIAN Come on. Let's have this one outside. Now!

MARK *(quietly)* Listen Brian, you're tired, you're a little drunk. Let's talk about this—

Scene Four

NARRATOR February eighteenth. Brian Tongue and Mark Bark-
Jones are in Sredny, a small outpost of civilisation on the
borders of Siberia. It is from here they will begin the long
walk into the icy wastes, of the Arctic.

Scene Five

Russian pub: Int.

Effects wind whistling past the open door (under).

MARK Out there...that's where we're going.

Silence but for wind.

INT I can't see anything.

MARK No. Quite.

BRIAN It gives you an idea, of what we'll be walking in. Zero visibility, fifty-mile-an-hour winds—

MARK All this waiting. To tell you the truth. I can't wait to get in it.

BRIAN Yea...you want to close the door Mark, you're letting all the heat out.

MARK Sorry...

Effects door slam. Crackling fire (under).

BRIAN That's better. Those Ruskies over there were looking a bit edgy...

Fade.

NARRATOR Episode Two. "Wind".

Scene Six

Russian pub. Int.

Effects crackling hearth.

INT So what's the delay?

MARK Wind.

INT Wind?

MARK That's right.

INT I thought you couldn't wait to get in it?

MARK Not this sort of wind.

INT It's the wrong sort of wind?

MARK Yes, remember what we'll be walking across is frozen ocean. This strong southerly wind simply shifts the ice, and us, southwards.

BRIAN We'd be like mice on a wheel. Going nowhere.

MARK Thinking positively, I suppose it's a blessing to have this period of acclimatisation, before setting off.

BRIAN Yea, out there it's minus twenty, and the twenty-mile-an-hour wind chill is taking it down to minus forty-eight. Pretty nippy.

MARK Put another log on the fire, Brian.

BRIAN Righto.

Effects hiss and stutter as log lands in flames.

INT So, will you be going outside soon, then?

MARK All in good time.

Effects plate and cutlery being placed on table.

MARK Thank you, Svetlana.

SVETLANA *(heavy accent)* You're velcome.

BRIAN We're aiming to set off two days from now.

MARK The Met Office says the wind'll be down by then. But if it's not, you know, that's nature for you. You can't rush it. Um, lovely soup.

Scene Seven

NARRATOR Also waiting keenly, back at HQ in Buckhurst Hill, is the "Antennae Giant", Graham Masters, who takes the time to make final adjustments to the geostationary satellite link-up.

Scene Eight

GRAHAM'*s house: Ext.*

Effects scrape, then sound of ladder against brick.

GRAHAM I've been Antennae Giant, ever since doing ham radio as a kid. The truckers called me Antennae Giant and it stuck...can you hold the bottom, of the ladder, Sandra—?

SANDRA Yea...

Effects GRAHAM *climbing ladder.*

SANDRA Sure it'll hold you, Graham? You can see why he's called Antennae Giant...

GRAHAM Hey, cheeky. It's cos of my forty-foot wotpole.

SANDRA You wish.

NARRATOR *(v/o)* We asked Graham to explain his role in the expedition.

Scene Nine

GRAHAM's *roof: Ext.*

Effects hammering.

GRAHAM *(as he works)* They're my boys. If they need an ear to talk to, I'm there on the radio waves. Sandra can come over, have a quiet catch up with Brian. If there's a bereavement in the family, I'll be straight on the radio to tell them of their loss. Mark's mother's not too well as we speak, so I might come in handy there. I'm a point of human contact, and I do my job to the best of my ability. *(Laughing)* Provided I get me money, know what I mean?

NARRATOR *(v/o)* Where does the money come from?

Scene Ten

GRAHAM's *house: Ext.*

Effort distant hammering, rattling ladder.

SANDRA Well, the sponsorship was my department. I did publicity for Mobberly Dramatic Society so I know what I'm doing. And I've got everybody from Norburton's suet to Flaxes Miny Mints—

GRAHAM *(shouting)* You got the gaffer tape, Sandra?

SANDRA *(shouting back)* It's in your pocket! Then there's Pat Franks at Altringham Camping and Leisure. Tampax Tampons. Dr John Clarson at Loughborough University, they're going to do some experiments for him—

GRAHAM *(distant)* Sandra, did you say Tampax—?

SANDRA ...into how the human body absorbs carbohydrate...

GRAHAM Tampax tampons?

SANDRA Ssh, Graham. Stick to your job, I'll stick to mine...

Scene Eleven

Snowy field: Ext.

Effects wind.

BRIAN Come on, Mark. Smile at the camera.

MARK I am smiling.

BRIAN Your hand's over the label. We've got to see it.

Effects click of camera shutter.

BRIAN What's that jacket you're wearing, Mark?

MARK Eh?

BRIAN For the listeners. Sooner you do it, sooner we can get back inside.

MARK It's a Dervly Fleece jacket with hood.

BRIAN What's so good about it?

MARK It's almost one hundred per cent breathable. It keeps an active body warm, but at the same time cool enough to prevent perspiration.

BRIAN Good. Now just move your hand up to your chest. I want to see you holding the Tampax tampons.

MARK What the hell are we supposed to do with them?

BRIAN Dunno. Just hold them.

Effects click of shutter.

Scene Twelve

NARRATOR We discovered that sponsorship, however, is only half the story. These are the facts. Mark's grandfather is Sir Clarence Bark-Jones, founding father of manufacturing conglomerate, Titan Trading. Titan Trading run numerous factories in central Africa. These factories have a workforce with an average age of ten.

Scene Thirteen

Russian pub: Int.

Effects crackling hearth, low Russian voices.

BRIAN Yea, Sandra's done a great job, eh Mark?

MARK She certainly has. Cheers!

BRIAN Cheers.

Effects vodka glasses slammed on table.

INT Mark, what does the name Titan Trading mean to you?

Pause.

INT We spoke to Zola, a worker in one of your grandfather's factories.

MARK My grandfather gave employment to—

INT She was twelve. She was making those little gloves that stretch to fit all hand sizes.

BRIAN Oh yea, they're very good, those—

INT She was paid ten pence per hour. Profits from Titan Trading go directly into your expedition fund.

MARK My grandfather gave employment to thousands of rural people—

INT Does little Zola know that she's funding a six-hundred mile trek to the North Pole?

MARK I think that little Zola would be proud and happy to contribute to such a good cause.

Effects glass on table.

Cheers.

BRIAN Steady, Mark, you know what happened last time.

MARK Aah, one more won't hurt.

Scene Fourteen

Russian pub: Int.

Effects crackling hearth.

MARK *snoring.*

INT What's the problem now? The wind's down. It's good conditions isn't it?

BRIAN Yea, but we're not going to rush into something like this. We're both pulling sleds almost three times our body-weight. We have to be one hundred per cent happy with all the equipment, or we risk letting a lot of people down. Mark's been having—

MARK *grunts in his sleep.*

BRIAN *(whispering)* ...a lot of trouble with his trouser zip. I've got a large metal ring attached to my zip around which cord can be fastened. Mark doesn't so he's had to fashion something from the top of a cola can. These things take time...

Scene Fifteen

Snowy field: Ext.

Effects wind blowing. Feet crunching on snow.

NARRATOR *(v/o)* February twenty-third. At last, seven days behind schedule, all is ready. Three years of preparation, expense, and obsession are about to be tested.

Effects blowing wind, all else is silence.

MARK I'm reminded of the words of the great Antarctic explorer Jean-Louis Etienne.

Pause.

"Now we are here, we have to go. We have spent three years with this crossing in our heads and now, sometimes, I feel like I am in a prison. A prison of our idea."

BRIAN Lighten up, Mark.

MARK Sorry.

INT So are you actually going to go now?

BRIAN Yea, we're all harnessed up. I've got my dad's lucky boots on!

INT Any word from Melissa?

MARK *(straining)* No...final good luck would've been nice...

BRIAN You got the harness on properly?

MARK Yea...perhaps if you give it a push...

Scene Sixteen

NARRATOR A worrying moment. Mark's load is proving too heavy to pull. Despite his smaller stature, Brian is able to shift his sledge without difficulty. After a few tense minutes, the mystery is solved.

Scene Seventeen

Snowy field: Ext.

INT I saw him put them under the tarpaulin.

MARK You stay out of it—

INT At least four bottles—

MARK What do you know about polar travel? Standing there in your little jumpsuit? They were bottles of antiseptic.

INT It looked like vodka.

MARK Well, we use vodka as antiseptic!

BRIAN Come on Mark, this happened last time.

MARK OK! So I thought it'd warm us up after a long day—

BRIAN And I like to listen to my CDs before bed, but I made the sacrifice 'cos we can't take any more weight!

MARK I'll get rid of them.

BRIAN Right.

MARK Can you stop recording?

BRIAN Yea, switch it off—

MARK That fluffy fucking mic in my face all the time. Just piss off—

Effects click as tape cuts out.

Scene Eighteen

NARRATOR Finally, with a determination and speed that belies the weight they are pulling, Brian and Mark are off, their figures cutting a lonely path across the Arctic tundra. From now on, their only contact with loved ones, the outside world, and with humanity itself, is through radio satellite link-up to Graham, the "Antennae Giant".

Scene Nineteen

Shed at HQ: Int.

Effects noise of radio transmission and interference.

GRAHAM This is Antennae Giant calling Walking Warriors, Over...

Effects radio buzz.

Well, the boys are about ten hours into their journey. They made contact briefly, said there was a slight problem, something about visibility, then I lost contact. Possibly they're in a "white out" situation. That's when the white snow merges with a white sky to form a disorientating world without definition. Still, that's something they're trained to cope with.

Effects transmission noise.

BRIAN *(distorted)* Walking Warriors to Antennae Giant—

GRAHAM Oh—

BRIAN —reading you loud and clear, over.

GRAHAM Roger that. Great to hear you two. How are you?

BRIAN Not too bad. Just a small problem.

MARK *(in background)* Big problem...

GRAHAM Visibility difficulties?

BRIAN That's right.

MARK Give me the – look. Brian's lost a lens.

GRAHAM Repeat that, over?

MARK A contact lens. He took his goggles off, fell over, and lost a lens.

Pause.

GRAHAM So that's the visibility problem, over?

MARK That's right.

GRAHAM He must have some spares?

MARK Forgot to pack them, over.

GRAHAM *(laughing)* What a laugh...

MARK Not at all funny, over.

GRAHAM So what's the solution, lads?

MARK We've radioed Sredny, Ruskies are sending a helicopter to pick us up, take us back to base.

GRAHAM Right. So that's the solution. Go back.

MARK That's right. Go back.

GRAHAM By helicopter.

MARK By helicopter.

GRAHAM Right.

MARK Right.

Scene Twenty

Russian pub: Int.

Effects crackling hearth, low Russian voices.

INT Brian and Mark, good to see you back so soon.

BRIAN Cheers.

INT So is this failure?

BRIAN Not at all. We've had a false start. All we have to do is wait here for a shipment of lenses, and then we're off!

MARK And it's not a bad place to wait.

BRIAN *(laughing)* He's got his vodka. He's happy.

Scene Twenty-One

NARRATOR Brian and Mark owe it to their sponsors to succeed beyond the settlement at Sredny. With ice melting as Arctic summer approaches, time is running out. On February twenty-fifth the second, and final attempt, is underway.

Scene Twenty-Two

Tent: Int.

Effects wind buffeting canvas, frying sounds.

BRIAN Well, here we are in the tent! End of day one! We've done a good ten miles, which is a great relief. I must say, they may be my dad's lucky boots, but it's great to get them off—

MARK Brian, who are you talking to?

BRIAN I'm recording—

MARK Oh right—

BRIAN Thanks to Altringham Camping and Leisure for the tent. Nice one, Pat! What's for dinner, Mark?

MARK Umm. I've boiled up those freeze-dried vegetables, now I'm frying that...cured sausage thing in suet.

BRIAN In what suet?

MARK Oh, Norburton's Suet.

Scene Twenty-Three

NARRATOR Perhaps spurred on by the weight of corporate finance that lies behind the expedition, the trek to the Pole is at last underway. Our interviewer now flies back to London, to follow progress from HQ, leaving it up to Brian and Mark, armed with their small tape recorder, to preserve their journey for others to hear.

Scene Twenty-Four

Tent: Int.

Effects radio buzz.

BRIAN Is it on?

MARK Yep...

GRAHAM *(distorted)* Antennae Giant calling Walking Warriors? Where's my wages? Your cheque bounced, over.

BRIAN Oh...is Sandra there, over?

Effects buzz.

SANDRA Hello, my love. How are you, over?

BRIAN Fine, love. Just about to have our dinner.

SANDRA Oh, have you recorded the suet jingle yet? For the sponsors. You've got the lyrics I wrote, over?

Effects buzz.

Norburton's gave us a lot of money.

MARK *(background)* Oh God.

BRIAN Alright love, how does the tune go?

SANDRA *hums the tune.*

Come on Mark, it'll be a laugh. Here we are...

Effects paper being uncreased.

"When you're cold and feeling funny". Come on, Mark. "When you're cold and feeling funny".

MARK "And you need warmth in your tummy".

BRIAN "And your legs they feel like lead".

MARK "You almost feel you're dead".

BRIAN "You need..."

BRIAN/MARK "Norburton's Suet, the suet for the lads. It gives you a glow—"

SANDRA Stop. Mark's got the rhythm wrong.

MARK Oh, God.

BRIAN Yea, come on Mark, it's in two-four time.

BRIAN/MARK "...the suet for the lads. It gives you a glow, when you're in the snow, and when you're feeling sad. You can... fry it, you can spread it, you can dunk it in the can, you can bung it in the cooker, you can whack it in the pan. You can rub it on your muscles, you can make it gel your hair, you can lubricate your armpits, or thwack it on your chair.

"Norburton's suet, the suet for the lads. We're off to the Pole, and we'll never be alone with Norburton's suet in our bags".

Effects silence, but for the wind flapping the tent.

BRIAN Sandra? What did you think?

MARK That was alright, wasn't it?

BRIAN Sandra?

Effects wind howls outside.

Effects wind gets louder and louder.

NARRATOR Next week, on *Beyond The Pole*.

Scene Twenty-Five

On ice: Ext.

Effects gale blowing.

BRIAN *(very faint)* Mark... Mark!

MARK Brian!

BRIAN *(distant)* Mark!

Scene Twenty-Six

Tent: Int.

Effects wind blustering canvas.

BRIAN It'll relieve the pressure!

MARK Don't bring that scalpel anywhere near me!

BRIAN There's a lot of pus in there and it's got to come out!

Scene Twenty-Seven

On ice: Ext.

Effects howling gale.

MARK *(shouting)* This is the last time I go exploring with someone who's got a circumcised penis!

Cut out.

NARRATOR Last week on *Beyond The Pole...*

End of episode

EPISODE THREE

Scene One

Snowy field. Ext.

Effects wind.

MARK —the pain, the misery, even death we endure for our loved ones, for our countrymen...and for humanity.

Pause.

BRIAN Lighten up, Mark.

Scene Two

Tent: Int.

Effects wind blustering tent.

BRIAN Come on Mark, it's in two-four time.

BRIAN/MARK Norburton's Suet, the suet for the lads—

Scene Three

On the ice: Ext.

Effects wind.

MARK That fluffy fucking mic in my face all the time. Just piss off—

Cut out.

Scene Four

Tent: Int.

Effects rustle of sleeping bag.

MARK Um... *(Cough)* It's about nine thirty am. Day twelve. We slept in this morning because it's a rest day.

Effects MARK *crawling out of the sleeping bag.*

We've done sixty miles in the last week, which isn't bad considering the terrain. Brian's outside doing his morning ablutions...

Effects zip being undone.

I've clipped one of our radio mics to my jacket, so I can take you outside. On a day like this...not much wind, sun's bright rays just bursting over the horizon...

(He sighs with satisfaction) There. Look at that. White. Ice. Virgin...ice. In all directions. Sometimes I feel so privileged...

Effects his feet on snow.

...it's such a beautiful sight.

Effects a squelch.

MARK Breathe it in.

He breathes deeply.

Umm...

Shorter sniffs. Then he yells.

MARK Bloody hell—

BRIAN *(distant)* What?

MARK Ugh.

BRIAN Sorry mate, couldn't hold out...

Pause.

Dicky tummy...

Effects click as mic being switched off.

NARRATOR Episode Three. "Shit".

Scene Five

Tent: Int.

Effects hiss of stove, frying.

BRIAN It's all this starchy, fatty food...freeze-dried meals...suet. I mean, fat is vital. We need the energy. But my guts aren't happy.

Effects an Elastoplast being unwrapped.

BRIAN Good thing about a day off, it gives my feet a rest.

MARK You were falling behind yesterday.

BRIAN Yea, I've got some nasty blisters, that's why I'm putting on a couple of plasters. I'll be fine tomorrow.

MARK OK—

BRIAN And I'll rub wax into my dad's boots in a bit.

MARK Good.

BRIAN Then I'll trim me beard.

MARK Great...

Scene Six

NARRATOR Brian and Mark have made up for a slow start to
their North Pole campaign by walking an average of eight
miles every day. Their well-deserved day of rest, however,
passes all too quickly. Can their luck continue as they head
across the frozen seas of the Nansen Basin? As he leaves the
tent, Mark again makes an unfortunate discovery.

Scene Seven

On the ice: Ext.

Effects slight wind. Tent zip being undone.

MARK I don't know what's the matter with Brian—

BRIAN *(approaching)* That's not mine. *(He kneels down)* I couldn't produce that.

MARK What are you saying?

BRIAN Well, it's too big for an arctic fox. Sniff it.

MARK I don't want to sniff it.

BRIAN *sniffs.*

BRIAN Umm. Powerful stuff. There's only one thing could do this.

MARK Not—?

BRIAN Yep. And look—

Effects slight squelch.

—it's recent. Get ready...we're in polar bear country.

Scene Eight

NARRATOR The polar bear. The fiercest and most formidable creature of the Arctic. It weighs in at around eight hundred kilograms, and can smell a potential meal from six miles. The bear is only one of the myriad dangers faced daily by Brian and Mark. For the moment, however, their luck seems to be holding.

Scene Nine

On the ice: Ext.

Effects wind.

MARK This is a good place to stop...have lunch...let Brian catch up...

Effects plastic being unwrapped.

We've just had to drag the sledges across miles of heavy rubble, but here in front...a frozen lead. *(He starts to eat)* Leads are passages of water, and when they're open, they're a pain, but frozen? We love 'em *(Shouting)* Come on Brian!

Effects BRIAN *approaching in the snow.*

BRIAN *(distant)* Is it lunchtime?

MARK Um...

Effects plastic being wrapped away.

MARK You've got the cereal bars, haven't you, Brian?

Effects BRIAN *collapsing on the snow.*

BRIAN *(out of breath)* Bloody cereal bars. Imagine we had...a roast dinner. That'd sort me out...

MARK Look at that. That'll cheer you up.

BRIAN Oh, brilliant...

MARK Yep...

BRIAN *(still breathless)* They're a bit like finding an oasis in a desert...well, an oasis in a frozen desert...but not a desert because there's lots of water. The reverse, or negative of an oasis, you could say...

MARK That's right, Brian. It's smooth, firm, and north facing. A polar superhighway.

BRIAN But an empty polar superhighway. No cars or lorries, getting in the way.

MARK Um. I suppose this puts us in the fast lane.

BRIAN But not too fast, eh Mark.

MARK You said your feet would be fine today.

BRIAN Yea, but it's more fun if we stay together. I'm sick of watching your arse all day.

MARK I'll go a steady pace. You've got to keep up.

BRIAN You've got to slow down. Come on.

MARK So the day off didn't help your blisters?

Pause.

MARK Your beard looks good, though.

Scene Ten

NARRATOR To reach the Pole, Brian and Mark must work as a
  team. Compromises must be made, and differing abilities
  catered for. Although Mark has the advantage of good health,
  he has not heard from Melissa, and must struggle on without
  the small shreds of comfort only a loved one can provide.

Scene Eleven

Tent: Int.

Effects wind buffeting canvas. Hiss of radio.

SANDRA *(distorted)* How are you my love, over?

BRIAN Smashing, love. How are you? What are you wearing, over?

SANDRA I'm fine, Brian. Repeat the other question, over?

BRIAN What are you wearing—?

MARK *sighs.*

BRIAN —just describe it to me, please, over.

SANDRA Tracky bottoms and that black v-neck from the sales.

BRIAN Right...umm...so you're not wearing that...red dress?

SANDRA No.

BRIAN Could you wear it next time...you know the one with the slit...up the side where your leg...pokes out...and you can see...umm...

MARK Oh please...

SANDRA I'll pretend I'm wearing it, if you like. Make out I've got those stay-ups on...

BRIAN Roger that—

Effects zip of tent opening.

BRIAN Where you going, Mark?

MARK What do you want me to do? Watch?

Effects zip of tent closing.

Scene Twelve

On the ice: Ext.

Effects wind.

NARRATOR *(v/o)* Day fourteen.

Effects plastic being unwrapped.

MARK Conditions stable. *(As he eats)* Hard ice, not much rubble. Brian's made three unscheduled toilet breaks, this being the third.

BRIAN *(distant)* My tummy's rough as a badger's arse.

MARK Brian showing the signs of suffering severe polar cuisine fatigue.

BRIAN *(approaching)* There's some more bear prints over there.

Effects plastic being scrumpled up and hidden.

BRIAN It must be pretty close.

MARK Yep. We'll need eyes in the back of our heads.

BRIAN You're ugly enough already, Mark.

MARK Ha ha...

BRIAN I can't wait to see a real live bear.

MARK The speed you're going, you won't have to wait long. They always go for the man at the rear.

BRIAN Like your mates in the T.A.?

MARK Huh, you're cheery today. Must be all that fun last night.

BRIAN Don't be jealous, Mark.

MARK I don't need cheap thrills to get through this. I'm just bored. This polar travel's becoming too easy. *(Shouting)*

Come on, you Arctic wilderness! Show us what you can do!
Let's have some action!

BRIAN Don't tempt fate, Mark...

Scene Thirteen

Shed at HQ: Int.

Effects hum of radio. **GRAHAM** *slurping tea.*

INT So, Graham, would you say they're very brave?

GRAHAM *(laughing)* Well, some would say they're just mad...

INT And are they?

GRAHAM What?

INT Are they mad, all these dangers for the sake of a British record?

GRAHAM They've been planning this for years. When you've got a dream...you do what it takes...

INT So bravery, then.

GRAHAM Yea...bloody brave.

Scene Fourteen

NARRATOR Despite Graham's denial, we discovered that Mark Bark-Jones, or "Barky" to his friends, underwent voluntary treatment in 1995, at a private mental hospital following a failed attempt to walk from Chatham to Shoeburyness. We asked if mental imbalance influenced Mark's decision to go to the Pole?

Scene Fifteen

Shed at HQ: Int.

GRAHAM Nah, he goes for stuff, and I admire him for that. His family's all the same, they go for gold. His great-grandfather went to explore Africa, ended up owning half of it. Exploring's in his blood.

Scene Sixteen

NARRATOR And so, it seems, is mental illness. His mother, Felicity, suffered a long-running obsession with Jeff Capes, champion strong man, which led eventually to his withdrawal from the public eye.

Scene Seventeen

On the ice: Ext.

Effects wind.

NARRATOR *(v/o)* Day sixteen.

BRIAN At last...in front of me... I have to keep my voice down...
is a remarkable sight. A polar bear. It's about four hundred
yards away...crossing a pressure ridge...and it's big, it's furry,
I think it's a male...like the lion is king of the jungle, the
polar bear is king of the polar...jungle...

Effects gunshot. Footsteps in snow. Another gunshot.

BRIAN You shot it.

Silence but for wind.

MARK It was us or the bear.

Scene Eighteen

Tent: Int.

Effects wind buffeting canvas. Spoon against pan.

MARK Nineteen hundred hours. Dinner's on the go. I'm boiling up some freeze-dried vegetables in oil. Lots of carbohydrate for energy...

BRIAN *(quietly)* I think you got off on it.

MARK What?

BRIAN The gun in your hand. Power over nature. That turned you on.

MARK *laughs.*

MARK It was self-defence.

BRIAN It was running away.

Silence.

BRIAN You love your gun.

MARK Dinner's ready, Brian—

BRIAN So you don't regret it?

MARK No.

BRIAN Bet you regret not being able to stuff it, and hang it over the mantelpiece...

MARK *(laughing nervously)* Eat up.

BRIAN Perv...

Scene Nineteen

NARRATOR Day seventeen. The journey must go on, but Brian's worsening health means they must pray for good conditions. With the death of the bear, however, their good luck seems to run out.

Scene Twenty

On the ice: Ext.

Effects gale-force winds, very severe.

MARK *(shouted)* Brian! Brian!

Effects mic being buffeted, then shielded.

I'm in a blizzard and... I was way ahead of Brian. So stupid... I should've kept with him! It came down so quick. Now, the silly bastard's out there, I don't know what to do... Brian... Brian!

Effects gale/blizzard increases.

BRIAN *(very faint)* Mark... Mark!

MARK Brian?

BRIAN *(getting nearer)* Mark?

MARK Over here Brian. Keep going.

Effects wind increasing.

Thank God...

Effects bearhug, backs being slapped.

I thought I'd lost you for good!

BRIAN Mark! You won't believe what happened out there...

Scene Twenty-One

Tent: Int.

Effects wind buffeting canvas.

Gorecki Symphony No.3 (under).

BRIAN I knew I could die. I couldn't see anything and then suddenly I saw a figure that looked like Mark, so I ran towards it...but then the figure disappeared and in the wind I heard my dad's voice...

MARK *(background)* It was my voice.

BRIAN It wasn't you. It was my dad. He was trying to tell me something...then the voice was gone.

Scene Twenty-Two

NARRATOR It is with some relief that Brian and Mark crawl into their tent that night. Mark suggests they take the next day off, and orders Brian to rest thoroughly. They are still less than a fifth of the way to the Pole. The death of the polar bear will prove an omen. The real test is yet to begin.

Scene Twenty-Three

Tent: Int.

Effects gas stove burning, spoon against pan.

BRIAN Normally now at home I'd be getting ready to have a nice bath, then off to line dancing class with Sandra, yet here I am, cooking suet with bad feet, headache and a dodgy tum, and I've just heard my dead dad in the snow, but I suppose we're having fun, and we always said we'd have fun, didn't we Mark. Mark?

Effects sleeping bag sounds.

MARK *(mouth full)* What?

BRIAN What are you doing under your sleeping bag?

Effects plastic bag being scrumpled.

MARK Nothing.

BRIAN What's that?

MARK What?

BRIAN That. What you've hidden under your bag?

Effects **BRIAN** *moving.*

MARK Get off! What I do in my sleeping bag is private. Will you... Get off –

Effects **BRIAN** *grabs plastic, unravelling it.*

BRIAN *(intake of breath)* Thai chicken sandwiches? Where the hell did you get those?

MARK Umm. The supermarket.

BRIAN Supermarket? What supermarket?

MARK *(embarrassed)* I've been storing them in an ice bucket...

BRIAN An ice bucket! You've been pulling ice across the ice?

MARK Yeah.

BRIAN I don't believe this.

Pause.

MARK I was saving the houmous and pastrami for you.

BRIAN How many have you got?

MARK About fifteen.

BRIAN So while I've been eating this suet shit...

MARK It's not shit it's Norburtons.

BRIAN Don't interrupt! You've been eating Thai chicken.

MARK Yea...

BRIAN What's this?

Effects rummaging at plastic.

Prawn?

MARK Sorry.

Pause.

MARK Do you want one?

Pause.

BRIAN *(a big sigh)* I'll have the houmous and pastrami.

Cut out.

NARRATOR Next week on *Beyond The Pole*...

Scene Twenty-Four

Tent: Int.

Effects wind blustering canvas.

MARK *(with a sigh)* This is beyond the call of duty. I am now rubbing the feet...the hairy feet...of a man who hasn't washed for a month...

Scene Twenty-Five

Tent: Int.

Effects loud growling.

BRIAN It's a bear! It's a bear!

Scene Twenty-Six

On the ice: Ext.

Effects howling wind.

MARK *(shouting)* This is the last time I go exploring with someone who's got a circumcised penis!

NARRATOR Last week on *Beyond The Pole...*

End of episode

EPISODE FOUR

Scene One

On the ice: Ext.

Effects gunshot.

BRIAN You shot it.

MARK It was us or the bear...

Scene Two

Tent: Int.

Effects wind blustering canvas.

BRIAN In the wind I heard my dad's voice...

MARK It was my voice.

BRIAN It wasn't you. It was my dad.

Scene Three

Tent: Int.

MARK Get off! What I do in my sleeping bag is private. Will you...get off!

Effects **BRIAN** *grabs plastic, unravelling it.*

BRIAN Thai chicken sandwiches? Where the hell did you get those?

Scene Four

Tent: Int.

Effects a storm blowing outside.

MARK Day thirty. Progress report. Weather is...cold. Outside is ice and snow, and cold, I am cold. Brian is also cold—

BRIAN Mark.

MARK Umm?

BRIAN Every day you record the same drivel. It's a waste of tape.

MARK It's a scientific record. Scott kept a journal and so am I.

BRIAN But he didn't keep saying it was cold, did he? He had a certain way with words.

MARK I'm keeping it simple. *(Continuing)* Snow everywhere. Ice everywhere. Relentless, icy—

BRIAN Mark for God's sake, record something interesting.

Pause.

BRIAN Let me... About one o'clock we—

MARK Thirteen hundred hours.

BRIAN Yes. We found sledge trails and human footprints in the snow.

MARK *(leaning in)* Norwegians. Rival expedition.

Effects cartridges being loaded.

BRIAN An hour later—

MARK Fourteen hundred hours.

BRIAN —we find more footprints.

MARK Polar bear.

BRIAN Yes, as they say...shoot one bear, and the mate'll come looking for revenge.

Effects gun being cocked.

What are you doing?

MARK We are no longer alone. We must be prepared. From now on, I will sleep with this loaded gun under my sleeping bag.

Effects gun being placed under bag.

BRIAN Is that for the Norwegians or the bear?

MARK *laughs slightly.*

Fade.

NARRATOR Episode four "Blood".

Scene Five

Tent: Int.

Effects radio buzz. Storm blowing.

GRAHAM *(distorted)* Evening boys, some interesting news to perk your night up, over.

MARK We know, Graham, over.

GRAHAM It's the Norwegians, they've caught you up, over.

MARK We know, over.

GRAHAM Even though they set off from Sredny a week after you did, over.

MARK We know, Graham. They must be taking re-supplies to keep the sledges lighter, over?

GRAHAM Big negative to that, Barky. They're an unsupported expedition, identical to yours...cept for one thing.

MARK What's that, over?

GRAHAM They're much faster.

Effects interference.

MARK Please don't call me Barky, over.

Scene Six

NARRATOR Brian and Mark have now been walking a month, and have covered two hundred and fifty miles. At this stage, they are far from the beginning, and a long way from the end. It is a critical time.

Scene Seven

Tent: Int.

Effects deep, frightening rumbles under the ice.

BRIAN Listen to that...

MARK God...!

NARRATOR *(voiceover)* The following night, the full moon brings a spring tide. With the currents of the Artic Ocean in turmoil, Brian and Mark experience their first ice-quake.

Effects ear-splitting cracking ice.

MARK Twenty-one hundred hours. The sea ice beneath our tent is being buffeted and squeezed by the—

BRIAN Tempestuous?

MARK —the tempestuous ocean. At any moment a pressure ridge could rise up, lifting our tent and hurling it like a...a...

BRIAN Damp sock—

MARK Like a damp sock, or the ice could split and we'd...we'd...

BRIAN Fall into the water and die.

MARK Yes...

BRIAN That's a bit more poetic, Mark.

Effects massive cracking ice.

MARK This is actually...terrifying...

Fade.

Scene Eight

Shed at HQ: Int.

Effects tea being poured.

GRAHAM Ta love.

SANDRA Don't spill it.

NARRATOR *(voiceover)* Meanwhile, back at HQ in Buckhurst Hill...

GRAHAM *(sighing)* Thirty-one bloody days I've been sat here, and me bum hurts. It's tough out there for the lads, but times like this I feel a bit of an unsung hero, know what I mean?

Effects slurp of tea.

GRAHAM Sandra, there's no sugar in this.

SANDRA I put two in. Give it a stir.

INT How about you Sandra? How are you coping?

SANDRA Um. It's a bit strange just watching his albums collecting dust. His Matey bubble bath by the taps in the bathroom unused, huh. The other day I found a hair on my pillow. That was nice.

Pause.

INT Has Melissa been over yet?

GRAHAM *(laughing)* Nah! You'd be lucky to get her out of Zone One! Mark did ask me to try and contact her, but she's never in—

Effects opening of a drawer, rummage of papers.

Though, I did get hold of a copy of Melissa's latest book...

SANDRA *(reading)* Rosie Beacham?

GRAHAM That's her whatsit...? Pseudonym. I thought I might read Mark a few extracts over the airwaves, remind him of home—

SANDRA Nice idea, cheer him up a bit...

Scene Nine

NARRATOR The following morning, ice as far as the eye can see has been pushed and squeezed into a vast expanse of five-foot ridges, walls, and drops. Pulling the sledges proves slow and painful, and Brian's right foot is showing the first signs of frostbite.

Scene Ten

Tent: Int.

Effects wind blustering tent.

MARK God.

BRIAN They look alright, don't they?

MARK Alright? They've gone purple.

BRIAN Don't be a drama queen, Mark. They'll be fine with a rub. *(Straining)* Give 'em a rub, eh, my back's a bit sore?

MARK I'm not touching them.

BRIAN Oh come on, Mark. Be a pal. For the sake of the expedition.

MARK *(with a sigh, he rubs)* This is beyond the call of duty. I am now rubbing the feet...the hairy feet...of a man who hasn't washed for a month...

BRIAN If they smell it's because—

MARK If they smell?

BRIAN It's cos my dad's lucky boots. The leather's old...

MARK Right.

BRIAN Here—

Effects zip being undone.

MARK What are you doing?

BRIAN I want to show—

MARK I don't want to see it!

BRIAN Look at it.

MARK Put it away. God! It's purple.

BRIAN It's really sore.

MARK Is it frostbitten?

BRIAN Must be. Let's have a look at yours.

MARK Eh?

BRIAN You're not circumcised like me, so you've got a protective covering—

MARK I don't think the people back home want to know about this—

BRIAN *(leaning into mic)* Day thirty-two. Discover I have a frostbitten penis.

MARK Alright, Brian.

BRIAN *laughs.*

MARK And I'm not rubbing it for you...

Scene Eleven

Tent: Int.

Effects radio buzz.

NARRATOR *(voiceover)* Day thirty-five.

GRAHAM *(distorted)* ...Samuel watched through the skylight, as her hands found Franco's thighs, two birch trunks thrusting between her—

Effects click as radio is switched off.

BRIAN I was enjoying that...

Pause.

MARK I was wondering...where have those Norwegians got to?

BRIAN They'll be miles ahead by now. They walk to school across this sort of terrain in Norway.

MARK They've an unfair advantage. I'm from Surrey.

BRIAN Umm. We've an ice rink in Altringham...

MARK Have you...?

BRIAN Yea...

Scene Twelve

NARRATOR Polar rivalry between British and Norwegians goes back for generations. On day thirty-seven, Brian and Mark at last come face to face with their Norwegian counterparts. They record the encounter for posterity.

Scene Thirteen

On the ice: Ext.

Effects wind.

Pause. A cough.

BRIAN Brian. Brian Tongue.

They half-heartedly shake hands.

TERJE Hello... Terje.

MARK Mark Bark-Jones. Pleased to meet you.

KETIL Ketil.

BRIAN Oh, as in Harvey?

KETIL Sorry?

BRIAN As in Harvey Keital?

KETIL No...

Effects wind.

Pause. BRIAN *rubs his hands together.*

BRIAN Chilly, isn't it.

Everyone grunts agreement.

Scene Fourteen

NARRATOR That evening, camping side by side in a unifying gesture, they all share a cup of tea in the British tent.

Scene Fifteen

Tent: Int.

Effects wind buffeting canvas. Tea being drunk.

BRIAN Aah. Lovely cup of tea, eh?

Grunts of agreement.

I tell you, those pressure ridges have done for me.

KETIL Perhaps your skis are too long. See ours? They don't get so stuck in rubble.

MARK Right...

TERJE And your tent is so old fashioned. Ours is light to carry and much less like an aircraft hanger—

MARK Thanks, but this design was good enough for Scott, so it's good enough for us.

TERJE *(laughing)* Ah yes, Scott.

Awkward pause.

KETIL Tell me, what boots do you have?

BRIAN My father's lucky boots will do me, thank you.

TERJE We use Nordic ski boots. Much more absorbent—

MARK *(muttering)* I suppose you've got plastic bags around your genitals?

KETIL Yes, it prevents crotch rot.

BRIAN Bollocks!

KETIL Yes...our bollocks.

Pause.

Effects click of recorder being switched off.

Scene Sixteen

NARRATOR Brian and Mark record no more of their encounter.
Fortunately for us, the Norwegians do.

Scene Seventeen

On the ice: Ext.

Effects wind.

MARK Go on! Name one great Norwegian explorer!

KETIL Fridjoff Nansen! At this moment we approach the Nansen ridge—

MARK It's the Arctic Mid-Ocean Ridge!

KETIL The Nansen Ridge! Then, of course, Amundson, who beat Scott to the South Pole!

BRIAN You're playing a dirty game, my lad.

Scene Eighteen

NARRATOR The race is on. For two days the rival teams struggle, with a mere half-mile of very frosty air between them, to gain the upper hand.

Scene Nineteen

On the ice: Ext.

Effects wind.

BRIAN *(distant shouting)* At least we can make good pop records!

MARK *(shouting)* "Nil point". I think you know what I'm saying.

BRIAN Yea. "Nil point". Can't even name one!

MARK *(shouting)* There's always A-ha!

BRIAN Yea, they were good!

MARK *(singing)* "Take on me".

BRIAN *(joining in)* "Take me on".

MARK *(shouting)* "Take us on!"

BOTH Take us on! You'll be gone!

They laugh in the distance.

Scene Twenty

NARRATOR Day forty-five sees both teams struggling in storm conditions. The Norwegians, however, are slowly and inexorably pulling ahead.

Scene Twenty-One

Tent: Int.

Effects wind. Canvas flapping.

BRIAN —this little piggy had roast beef and this little piggy had none, and this little piggy—

MARK —might have to come off.

BRIAN Don't be daft. Sandra always says my toes look funny.

MARK Brian, your blood vessels have frozen. That is a real danger sign.

BRIAN Just pass me a sandwich, Mark.

MARK *sighs.*

MARK We'll never catch them up at this rate.

BRIAN So amputating my foot's the answer, is it? We're not here to have a race, we're here to have fun. Now lighten up and give us one of those Thai chicken...

Effects growling bear outside tent.

MARK Shit!

Effects huge roaring sound.

BRIAN It's a bear, it's a bear!

Effects panic sounds, scrambling around, looking for gun.

Quick Mark, where is it?

MARK Can't find it—

BRIAN Where's the gun!

MARK Shit, I left it in the sledge.

BRIAN Mark!

Effects growls, very, very loud.

MARK Give me back that sandwich!

BRIAN What the hell are you doing?

MARK Just stay here, this one is mine!

BRIAN Mark...

Effects zip being opened. Furious growling for a moment, then fading into distance. Silence but for wind.

(Whispered) Mark?

Scene Twenty-Two

Tent: Int.

BRIAN *(whispered)* My mind is filled with images of Mark, torn from limb to limb. His head...possibly three metres from his body...and his feet, perhaps a few miles away. Without toes...

Effects zip being undone.

MARK Hi.

BRIAN You're alive!

MARK Thank God he likes Thai chicken...

Scene Twenty-Three

Tent: Int.

Effects wind buffeting canvas. Radio buzz.

GRAHAM *(distorted)* Congratulations boys—

SANDRA *(distorted)* —well done, Brian. I'm very proud, over.

NARRATOR *(voiceover)* Brian and Mark have now walked three hundred miles. As the crow flies, they are halfway to the Pole.

BRIAN Thank God for Mark. If he hadn't led that bear away last night...we wouldn't be here, over.

GRAHAM Shame about those Norway boys, over.

BRIAN Are they OK, over?

GRAHAM Yea, the bear mauled them a bit, but they'll live. They've been airlifted to safety. D'you think it was the same bear, over?

Pause.

MARK There's a lot of them about, over.

Scene Twenty-Four

NARRATOR Survival in the Arctic depends on three things. One, experience, two, equipment, and, three, luck. The Norwegians had the first two, but were perhaps unfortunate in ever meeting Brian and Mark.

Scene Twenty-Five

Tent: Int.

Effects radio buzz.

GRAHAM *(distorted)* Well done anyway, lads. Oh Mark, I rang Melissa to tell her the good news, but she'd gone away for the weekend, so here's a little extract from "Horn of Desire" to keep you going... "Through a steamy haze, Sandy saw the towel fall from Franco's..."

Effects distort and transmission noise.

BRIAN Shit...

Effects BRIAN trying to adjust frequency.

GRAHAM ...a bead of sweat slid down her quivering...

Effects transmission whine.

MARK Shouldn't we be recording our journal?

Effects distort.

BRIAN This is better than you wittering on about ice.

Effects BRIAN adjusting frequency.

BRIAN This stuff might teach you something.

MARK Brian, I taught her everything she knows.

Effects transmission whine.

GRAHAM ...his leather-bound body, nipples pierced with eagle claws, flinched as she landed the bull whip on his—

Effects MARK switches off the radio.

BRIAN *(quietly)* You taught her very well...

Effects click as tape recorder switched off.

Shostakovich (under).

NARRATOR Next week on *Beyond The Pole*...

Scene Twenty-Six

Tent: Int.

Effects wind blustering canvas.

MARK Say it! Into the mic!

Pause.

BRIAN Mark has the best beard.

Scene Twenty-Seven

Tent: Int.

BRIAN I saw a mermaid. She turned around...she had the face of my dad.

Scene Twenty-Eight

On the ice: Ext.

Effects howling wind.

MARK This is the last time I go exploring with someone who's got a circumcised penis!

Cut out.

NARRATOR Last week, on *Beyond The Pole.*

End of episode

EPISODE FIVE

Scene One

Tent: Int.

Effects wind.

BRIAN —this little piggy had roast beef and this little piggy had none, and this little piggy—

MARK —might have to come off.

Scene Two

Tent: Int.

GRAHAM *(distorted)* ...a bead of sweat slid down her quivering...

Effects transmission whine.

BRIAN Shit...

Scene Three

On the ice: Ext.

Effects wind.

BRIAN *(distant)* At least we can make good pop records!

MARK *(distant)* "Nil point". I think you know what I'm saying!

Scene Four

Tent: Int.

Effects wind buffeting canvas.

Long pause. The odd cough, movement.

NARRATOR *(voiceover)* Day sixty-five. April twenty-ninth.

Another very long pause.

BRIAN *(just awake)* Mark? Mark...are you taping this?

MARK Umm.

Pause.

BRIAN We're not saying anything.

MARK It's our duty...to keep a thorough log...to record events as they happen.

Pause.

BRIAN Nothing's happening. What's the point...

Pause.

MARK We should get up.

BRIAN I can't.

MARK It's eight o'clock. Come on.

Pause.

BRIAN *sings "SUMMER LOVING" BY JIM JACOBS AND WARREN CASEY*

MARK Brian, not now.

BRIAN Let's sing. Our morning song. It always gets us going. *(Singing)*

MARK *and* **BRIAN** *continue to sing "SUMMER LOVING" BY JIM JACOBS AND WARREN CASEY*

MARK Why am I always Olivia bloody Newton John?

BRIAN 'Cos you sound like a girl. C'mon.

As they get up.

BOTH *Continue to sing "SUMMER LOVING" BY JIM JACOBS AND WARREN CASEY*

Effects tent zip.

Their singing peters out.

NARRATOR *(voiceover)* As Brian and Mark step outside the tent, they see nothing but water. The stretch of ice upon which they camped, has broken off from the ice sheet, leaving them adrift on the Arctic Ocean.

Effects wind.

MARK Great.

BRIAN *sighs.*

BRIAN I knew we should've stayed in bed.

Fade.

NARRATOR Episode Five. "Fucked"

Scene Five

Shed at HQ: Int.

Effects radio buzz.

GRAHAM Morning boys, over.

BRIAN *(distorted)* Morning Graham.

Effects buzz.

NARRATOR *(voiceover)* Day sixty-eight.

GRAHAM It's a lovely spring morning over here. The sun's shining through the window, and Sandra's sitting here, and she's looking lovely in her yellow outfit like a little daffodil. How is it for you two over?

Effects buzz.

BRIAN No comment. Over.

Effects **GRAHAM** *taking biscuit out of packet.*

GRAHAM You still drifting, over?

BRIAN Copy that. We're running low on food...just cereal bars... and suet. Still, can't complain.

GRAHAM *(eating)* What are you...sorry, mouth's full of flapjack... what are you up to today, Brian?

BRIAN Just staying in the tent today. Mark's outside doing some target practice, over.

Effects interference.

GRAHAM Your bird's trying to persuade me to go line dancing with her—

SANDRA *(pleading)* Oh go on. *(Into mic)* Brian? Tell Graham to come dancing. It's no fun on my own. Over.

Effects buzz.

BRIAN Replacing me already, over?

SANDRA Brian, are you alright?

BRIAN Didn't mean that. Sorry, love...

Scene Six

NARRATOR Arctic summer is rapidly approaching. With Brian
and Mark drifting helplessly over the Fram Basin, and the
North Pole still one hundred and thirty miles away, time
is running out.

Scene Seven

Tent: Int.

Effects wind buffeting.

BRIAN *(into mic)* Day seventy-two. This is a blessing in disguise. Sheltering from the relentless minus seventy wind chill can only help my mental and physical condition.

MARK *(leaning in)* It doesn't help us get to the Pole, does it...

BRIAN I'm dosed to the eyeballs with painkillers. Mark feels amputation may be the only option left for my frostbitten toes.

MARK A bit of frostbite is not going to get between us and the North Pole.

BRIAN *(deep breath)* Even simple tasks have become difficult. Going to the loo is agony what with my frostbitten—

MARK That might have to come off too.

BRIAN *sighs deeply.*

BRIAN I'm not enjoying this trip any more, Mark.

MARK You need to get out more. Keep busy. What about doing some of those experiments for Doctor Clarson?

BRIAN What experiments?

MARK You know...the ones we promised...for Loughborough Uni...

BRIAN Into how the human body copes with Arctic conditions?

MARK Umm.

BRIAN Look at me. There's your answer. It doesn't.

Fade.

Scene Eight

Tent: Int.

Effects wind buffeting.

NARRATOR *(voiceover)* Day seventy-three.

BRIAN Measure it right from the top...

MARK Keep still—

BRIAN How long is it?

MARK Six centimetres. Now measure mine...

NARRATOR *(voiceover)* Brian and Mark struggle to keep busy, taking advantage of the empty days to collect data.

MARK Four? It's more than that.

BRIAN *(into mic)* May seventh. Mark's beard is approximately four centimetres long...only.

MARK This isn't what Doctor Clarson meant...

BRIAN Look how thick mine is! A month ago it was a Bill Oddie, now it's a Grizzly Adams!

MARK *(muttered)* I'm going to polish my gun.

Scene Nine

Shed at HQ: Int.

GRAHAM *sipping tea.*

INT So how worried are you?

GRAHAM Well, it's not looking good. They can definitely kiss goodbye to breaking the British record. As for Brian – *(whispering)* we can't get the truth...he might be on his last legs, for all we know.

SANDRA *(offstage)* Come and try these on!

INT What's happening?

GRAHAM Well, I've decided to attend line dance class with Sandra. I like to keep things happy at home, as well as supporting the boys on the ice.

SANDRA *(entering)* I've found you out Brian's goat hide engraved boots. Size eight. That's right, isn't it?

GRAHAM Thereabouts.

INT How do you feel, Sandra?

SANDRA I'm looking forward to it.

INT Not the line dancing. About Brian.

GRAHAM Brian'll be fine! Look at these boots! *(Sings a line from "COWBOY SONG" BY THIN LIZZY).*

SANDRA *(laughing)* You're a daft one, daft and barmy.

Scene Ten

NARRATOR One week later, Brian and Mark still drift, jostling with pack ice and floes in a vast expanse of freezing ocean. The beard growing competition, meanwhile, is hotting up.

Scene Eleven

Tent: Int.

Effects wind buffeting.

MARK Go on. Measure it and weep!

BRIAN I don't believe it! So, it's grown six centimetres in one week?

MARK Yep. *(Into mic)* fourteenth of the fifth. Mark now has the longest beard. Say I've got the best beard.

BRIAN I'm not saying—

MARK Say it! Into the mic!

Pause.

BRIAN Mark has the best beard.

MARK Right.

BRIAN You always have to win, don't you.

MARK No, I don't...

BRIAN You're obsessed...

MARK No, I'm not...

Scene Twelve

NARRATOR Doped on painkillers, Brian has been easily deceived.
Later that day, he discovers Mark artificially enhanced his
beard with strands pulled from a woollen sock.

Scene Thirteen

On the ice: Ext.

Effects wind.

MARK *(into mic)* To be able to handle a weapon with skill and precision is vital to Arctic survival. This little baby is the seven-point-six-two S.L.R., self-loading rifle, as used by the marines. *(Shouting)* Brian, I'll shout pull, then you throw the snowballs into the air!

BRIAN *(distant)* Okay.

MARK *(into the mic)* Now obviously you won't be able to see me hit the balls but you can appreciate the power and sound of the weapon. *(Shouting)* Ready?

BRIAN *(even more distant)* Ready?

MARK *(shouting)* Pull!

Effects loud gun shot.

Silence.

MARK Pull!

Effects gun shot.

BRIAN *(shouted)* Watch it, Mark, put it down now that's enough.

MARK Don't be stupid.

BRIAN It's wasting ammunition, stop it now!

Effects sound of gun being loaded.

MARK Come on! Let's rock and roll!

Effects gun shot.

BRIAN *(nearer)* I didn't throw anything then.

MARK You did. I was just too quick for you.

BRIAN Give me the gun now.

MARK No.

BRIAN Give it to me.

Silence.

Effects sound of struggle ending in gun shot.

Scene Fourteen

Shed at HQ: Int.

Effects radio buzz.

GRAHAM *(mouth full)* You gotta make a decision, lads. Maybe it's time to call it a day, over.

MARK *(distorted)* We're not stopping, over.

GRAHAM Copy that, Mark. How is Brian, over?

Effects buzz.

MARK He's being a drama queen, the bullet was nowhere near him. What are you eating?

GRAHAM Cheeseburger, mate. I'd offer you some but you're a couple of thousand miles away. So you're gonna carry on, over?

Pause.

MARK Roger that, over.

GRAHAM Suit yourself. I'm off for a hot bath, over and out.

Effects GRAHAM *switching off radio.*

GRAHAM He's off his head...

GRAHAM *goes off to bathroom.*

Scene Fifteen

Shed at HQ: Int.

Effects radio interference.

NARRATOR *(voiceover)* Day eighty-one. Brian makes the decision to split up with Sandra.

BRIAN *(distorted)* It's just not working, over.

SANDRA *(upset)* But why?

Effects long radio hiss.

BRIAN I never get to see you.

SANDRA But you're in the Pole.

BRIAN I know but...you see... I can't handle long-distance relationships.

Effects long radio hiss.

SANDRA Have you met someone?

BRIAN No, love.

SANDRA I don't understand.

BRIAN Look it's just... I need some space.

SANDRA You're in the Arctic! How much space do you need?

Fade.

Scene Sixteen

Tent: Int

Effects wind.

BRIAN *(whispering)* Three weeks now...we've been drifting. I'm frightened. My whole body feels frozen. I'm worried about Mark. He just sits outside the tent polishing his gun and whistling... *(He coughs)* I hope you hear this Sandra. I always loved you. I know you've got Graham now, but I split with you because I wanted to spare you. I'm dying, that's the truth—

Effects zip of tent being opened.

MARK Brian! Let's get packed!

BRIAN Eh?

MARK We've joined the ice sheet. The expedition's on again!

BRIAN *(quietly)* Great...

Scene Seventeen

NARRATOR Driven by a new energy, Mark's sledge is packed and ready in twenty minutes. An hour later, joined by Brian, they are ready to make the crossing onto firmer ice.

Scene Eighteen

On very thin ice: Ext.

Effects cracking ice. Enormous splash.

MARK Brian?

Effects splashing.

BRIAN *has fallen in.*

Effects splashing.

He's in the water...splashing about.

BRIAN Help!

MARK I'll just put—

Effects mic being put on ground. Splashing.

(Shouting) Here...hold on! Grab this!

Effects splashing.

Scene Nineteen

Tent: Int

Effects burning stove. Wind.

BRIAN *(shivering)* I need to...

MARK Lie still.

BRIAN Record this...my father was there...

MARK Where?

BRIAN In the sea. I saw a mermaid, who had the most beautiful body. She turned around and I thought that my heart had stopped... She had the face of my dad. My dad was a mermaid. He pulled me to safety, a hand from nowhere—

MARK It was my hand. I pulled you out—

BRIAN *(angry)* My dad was there...he was pointing to his tail, trying to tell me something really important...

MARK Sleep now, Brian, busy day tomorrow.

Scene Twenty

Shed at HQ: Int

Effects radio hiss.

BRIAN *(distorted)* Walking Warrior calling Antennae Giant, over.

Effects interference.

GRAHAM Bugger...

Effects **GRAHAM** *sitting down.*

(Sighing) Reading you Walking Warrior. Make it brief, as I've got a pint of ale waiting at the pub, over.

BRIAN Are you meeting Sandra, over?

GRAHAM I'm just trying to cheer her up, mate. She's upset.

BRIAN I've been in the water. I don't think I'm going to make it.

GRAHAM *(muttering)* Bloody hell. Shall I order a helicopter?

Effects buzz.

BRIAN Mark's outside. He doesn't know I'm calling you...

GRAHAM We'll get a copter out there straight away.

Scene Twenty-One

NARRATOR For Brian, this seems the end of the line. He does not realise, however, that while drifting on the ice pack, a Northerly wind has pushed them a mere eighty miles from the Pole.

Scene Twenty-Two

Tent: Int.

Effects wind buffeting tent.

BRIAN *coughs and shivers in background.*

MARK Day eighty-two. The wind is down to twenty knots, and we're clear for our final push.

BRIAN *gurgles.*

Brian is taking some much needed rest...

Effects distant helicopter.

Tonight I will myself, perform the amputation on Brian's frost-bitten limbs...

Effects helicopter closer.

BRIAN *(muttering)* Thank God.

MARK What's that?

Effects zip being opened.

BRIAN I got Graham to radio Sredny. I can't go on. It's over, Mark.

MARK But we're almost there!

Effects gun being loaded.

BRIAN I need help.

MARK We don't need help. We're unsupported! Unsupported, understand?

MARK *goes outside.*

Effects helicopter above tent.

(Shouting) Go away!

Effects gun shot.

BRIAN Oh shit...

MARK That's a warning! We don't need you!

Effects gun shot.

That's another. Right then!

Effects gun shots. Broken propeller sounds, followed by huge crash.

Effects silence but the wind.

Fade.

Shostakovich (under).

NARRATOR Next week on *Beyond The Pole*...

Scene Twenty-Three

On the ice: Ext.

Effects gale blowing.

After a long time.

MARK This is the last time I go exploring with someone who's got a circumcised penis!

Cut out.

Shostakovich.

NARRATOR Last week on *Beyond The Pole*...

End of episode

EPISODE SIX

Scene One

On thin ice: Ext.

Effects splashing.

MARK Brian has fallen in...

Effects more splashing.

MARK He's in the water...splashing about...

Scene Two

Tent: Int.

Effects wind.

BRIAN *(whispering)* Eighty days we've been out on the ice...
my frostbite is agony and I can never...get dry. *(Sighing)*
This trip's no fun any more.

Scene Three

On ice: Ext.

MARK We're unsupported! We don't need you!

Effects helicopter. A gun shot.

(Shouting) That's a warning! Right then!

Effects gun shots. Broken propeller sounds. Crash.

Scene Four

Tent: Int.

Effects wind buffeting.

Grunts, movements in sleeping bags.

BRIAN Night time...day eighty-two.

MARK *(muttering)* Move over...can you...

RUSSIAN Mudac.

BRIAN Sharing the tent with three Russian crewmen, shot down yesterday by Mark.

Annoyed sighs.

It's a bit cramped in here...good thing is, it's cosy, so, after being in the water yesterday, it's probably the best thing for me.

MARK *(irritated)* This is ridiculous... I can't sleep with this fat Russian...in my face...

RUSSIAN Mudac.

Pause.

MARK Don't you speak English?

Russian muttering.

RUSSIAN Mudac.

MARK I know you speak English. Let's be civil.

RUSSIAN I said wanker.

MARK Oh...

Fade.

NARRATOR Episode six. "Finished".

Scene Five

Tent: Int.

Effects wind on tent.

Russian muttering.

BRIAN *(quietly)* You're lucky, Mark, you could've killed them. There's gonna be consequences.

MARK What do you think the Royal Geographical Society will say?

BRIAN It's all over, Mark.

MARK No.

BRIAN My feet are that swollen I can hardly get my dad's boots on—

MARK Just one last burst Brian.

BRIAN We've no food—

MARK We've enough cereal bars to last two weeks, if we economise.

BRIAN You've just shot down a Russian naval helicopter!

MARK We knew there'd be challenges. That's what it's about! It's about doing it for Britain.

BRIAN Bugger Britain.

Pause.

MARK I'll go on alone then.

BRIAN *sighs.*

RUSSIAN Mudac.

MARK Brian...can you switch—

Effects click as tape is switched off.

Scene Six

NARRATOR The following day, a gun-ship helicopter picks up the stranded Russians, and with the North Pole eighty miles away, Brian and Mark make the decision, against advice, to carry on. After four days struggling to haul the sledges in storm conditions, the wisdom of that decision is under question.

Scene Seven

Shed at HQ: Int.

Effects radio crackle.

BRIAN *(distorted)* This is Walking Warriors, can you hear me, over?

GRAHAM Very faintly Brian, how's it going?

BRIAN It's going nowhere, over.

GRAHAM Look, you can stop all this at any time Brian, over.

SANDRA *(in background)* Tell him about Tampax.

GRAHAM Brian. The tampon team are going to take away their sponsorship unless you promote the product in some way, over.

BRIAN Yea, yea. How is Sandra?

SANDRA *(in background)* I don't want to talk to him.

BRIAN Is she there, Graham?

SANDRA *(in background)* Tell him no.

GRAHAM She...er...yes, she is.

SANDRA Graham!

BRIAN You've really moved in quick there mate.

GRAHAM *sighs.*

BRIAN I'm surprised you're not wearing my pyjamas, over.

GRAHAM Don't be stupid, over.

SANDRA *(into mic)* At least he's here, keeping me company instead of miles away being grumpy and angry.

Effects click as radio switched off.

GRAHAM Sandra...

Scene Eight

NARRATOR Over the next two days, the minus eighty degree wind-chill saps their energy, and Brian's painful feet force a rest every few hundred yards. Day eighty-nine, and the situation has become critical.

Scene Nine

Tent: Int.

Effects gale outside.

MARK We are weak, recording...is difficult. Every day, Brian hobbles around like an old man.

BRIAN I should have gone back with the Russians.

MARK To what? Failure?

BRIAN Back to Sandra.

MARK What's the point? She's moved on now.

Silence but for gale outside.

BRIAN This is it, then...

BRIAN *gets up.*

Effects zip opening.

MARK Where are you going?

BRIAN Out. For a bit...

Effects zip closing behind him.

MARK I'm reminded of Scott's final entry in his journal. "Had we lived, we should have a tale to tell of the hardihood, endurance, and courage...which would have stirred the heart of every Englishman. These rough notes and our dead bodies must tell the tale..."

Slight laugh.

If Brian were here...he'd tell me to lighten up. But he's not... he's gone...

Fade.

NARRATOR Half an hour later, Brian is back.

Scene Ten

Tent: Int.

"We Are The Stars"/Jan Garbarek (under).

Effects wind battering tent.

BRIAN I just kept walking. I could see a shimmer of light cutting across the ice forming a kind of tunnel. I ran towards it but then stopped. In front of me, was my dad. He was smiling from ear to ear. He pointed to his boots and then he spoke, "Take em off lad, it's time to take em off. They weren't lucky for me, they'll never be lucky for you". It was then I realised.

Pause.

MARK What?

BRIAN Think about it, these boots have always brought me trouble. I fell over and lost a lens, I nearly died in a blizzard, got frostbite in my toes, then I tripped into the ocean. This is what he's been trying to tell me all along.

MARK Didn't your dad fall to his death wearing those boots?

BRIAN Yeah, he did.

MARK Well, did you never suspect they might be unlucky?

BRIAN I never really thought about it like that...

Scene Eleven

NARRATOR The following day, wearing back-up footwear from the sledge, Brian buries his father's lucky boots in the snow. With a renewed energy and vigour, the explorers press on, the North Pole once again firmly in their sights.

Scene Twelve

Kitchen at HQ: Int.

Effects spoon against pan, beating eggs.

INT I see you're baking a cake.

GRAHAM Yea, the lads said...you know, get ready, I think we might make it, and Mark asked me to get in touch with Melissa, tell her he's nearly there. So we're sorting out a little party. I'm baking a cake... I'm gonna put lots of white icing on the top, y'know...so it's like covered in snow?

INT What if they don't make it?

GRAHAM Well? I'll still get to eat the cake. Can't lose. *(He laughs)* But yea. It looks like they might actually make it.

INT Amazing.

GRAHAM Yea. It is frankly.

Scene Thirteen

NARRATOR For seven days Brian and Mark push ever nearer to the Pole. The closer they get, the more pain is forgotten, and the faster they walk. On day ninety-two, they discover a newly frozen lead, heading north.

Scene Fourteen

On the ice: Ext.

Effects wind.

MARK Today is the day...we should have broken the record. The British record...but we're still a few days away.

BRIAN What's important now is we get there—

MARK Yea...

BRIAN It's amazing...it's like we're being pushed by an invisible hand—

MARK We're certainly moving fast—

BRIAN A hand from nowhere.

MARK Whatever...

Scene Fifteen

On the ice: Ext.

Effects wind. Footsteps on ice, sledges being dragged.

NARRATOR *(voiceover)* Day ninety-five.

MARK *(out of breath)* We've switched the radio mics on... because...we've actually gone beyond the North Pole, and we're now retracing our steps. I've got the beacon in my hand...and it's just given a reading of eighty-nine, fifty-nine fifty-nine north.

BRIAN *(huffing)* We're nearly – I can't really describe my...it's a blur... I feel like a donkey...with a carrot...only an icy carrot...

MARK Brian, don't try to speak, just keep walking...another half mile...we are so close...

Establish and fade.

Scene Sixteen

At the Pole: Ext.

Effects wind.

Whooping, screams.

BRIAN Give us a hug mate. We did it.

MARK Yea...well done.

They slap each other on the back.

We didn't break the record, but fuck it!

BRIAN We're stood here, in one piece, as we said we would be. *(Shouting)* We made it! Come on, there's something we got to do.

MARK *whoops into the wind.*

Effects unpacking something from the sledge.

MARK The flag! Get out the flag!

Effects plastic being unwrapped.

What's this?

BRIAN Oh...

MARK Where did you get this?

BRIAN In the shop. It was all wrapped up.

MARK Brian...

BRIAN Look, there's a picture of a Union Jack on the packet.

MARK Well, it's not a Union Jack is it? It's...got yellow and black stripes...and...it's a bloody German flag.

Pause.

BRIAN Bollocks.

MARK We can't put that up!

BRIAN We've got to put something up.

Effects flag flapping in the breeze.

Fade.

Scene Seventeen

Shed at HQ: Int

Effects can being opened. Low murmur of voices.

NARRATOR *(voiceover)* Meanwhile, back at Buckhurst Hill, the party waits for news.

GRAHAM Yea, it's a great turnout. Sandra, the sponsors... Pat Franks from Altringham Camping and Leisure over there—

INT I understand you've even heard from Melissa?

GRAHAM Through her solicitor, yea, but I'll keep that quiet, for now...

INT She's filing for divorce?

GRAHAM Yea, but he's at the Pole. Bad news like that can wait.

Effects radio distort.

MARK Walking Warriors calling Antennae Giant, over?

GRAHAM Antennae Giant, reading you loud and clear. State your position, over?

MARK On top of the world, over.

Cheers.

Effects champagne cork being popped.

GRAHAM Listen to this...hear that, guys? Everyone's here...loads of journalists. Press interest has been amazing since you shot down the copter, you're famous, lads! Are you having a good time, over?

More cheering.

MARK Yea, we've got one last teabag to share. Is Melissa there, over?

Pause.

GRAHAM No, mate...she's not. She can't be here 'cos she's in Greece with some bloke who's gonna put her books onto film, but she sends a message.

Pause.

She says well done.

Effects hiss.

But there are a few lovely ladies from Tampax who fancy a word...

Scene Eighteen

At the Pole: Ext.

Effects wind.

BRIAN It's gotta be done, Mark. For the sponsors.

MARK In front of this?

BRIAN Any flag'll do. Come on, smile!

Effects shutter click.

Now take one of me.

MARK Right...get further in.

BRIAN I'm not covering up the flag...

MARK Come on—

BRIAN Oh bloody hell...

MARK What?

BRIAN I've got a nosebleed.

MARK *(laughing)* You're falling apart, Brian.

BRIAN Must be a bit excited.

MARK Wipe it on the flag.

BRIAN Mark!

MARK No, hang on...don't move.

Effects paper being unwrapped.

BRIAN No. I can't.

MARK Shove it up your nose.

BRIAN I can't stand with a tampon up my nose!

MARK Go on, it'll stem the flow...smile...

Effects click of shutter.

That'll keep Tampax happy.

Scene Nineteen

Shed at HQ: Int.

Effects hiss of radio.

GRAHAM *(slurred)* Copy that, Sredny. Roger and out...

NARRATOR *(voiceover)* Bad news. The relationship between our explorers and the Russians is under strain. Having had one helicopter destroyed, they are refusing to send another to return Brian and Mark to Sredny.

Squeals and laughter.

SANDRA *(to GRAHAM)* Give us a dance you big soft cowboy!

GRAHAM *(shouting)* Get a bit of "Whacko Jacko" on Colin.

INT Graham...are you going to tell Brian and Mark the news from Sredny?

"BEAT IT"/Jackson.

GRAHAM *(shouting, dancing)* In a minute...you're a good little mover Sandra.

SANDRA *(dancing)* Ta...

INT It seems both Brian and Mark have suffered strains...with loved ones...during this expedition...

GRAHAM Well, that's the price you pay. Come closer Sandra, I want to tell you something...

SANDRA Don't be daft, we're having a dance—

GRAHAM Come on Sandra, stop mucking about, give us a kiss—

SANDRA Graham, stop it.

Drunken scuffle.

GRAHAM Brian'll never know—

SANDRA Stop it!

SANDRA slaps GRAHAM.

Now get off and stay off!

SANDRA goes.

Pause.

GRAHAM How about you? Fancy a dance?

INT Well—

GRAHAM Loosen up, eh, and put down that microphone.

INT *(laughing)* Oh, alright—

Effects click as mic is switched off.

Scene Twenty

NARRATOR After two years of preparation, and ninety-five days of struggle, Brian Tongue and Mark Bark-Jones have made it to the North Pole. The quest is over. The problems, however, are not.

Scene Twenty-One

At the Pole: Ext.

Effects wind.

MARK Well...

BRIAN Yep...

Silence but for wind.

MARK Funny. You feel it should be special in some way...the North Pole.

BRIAN Yea...like there should be something at the end, like a bar, perhaps. Get a nice Pole burger and a Pole Coke...

Silence but for wind.

MARK But actually it's no different to anywhere else in the Arctic. Ice stretching in all directions. Tell you the truth, I'm sick of the sight of it.

BRIAN Still, it's amazing to think, down there below our feet... the world is revolving...

MARK Yea...yea it is.

Pause.

Question is, how are we going to get back to it?

Effects wind picking up.

End of episode

SOUND/EFFECTS

Effects spitting, frying fat (p2)
Effects thud of feet, hum of running machine (under) (p3)
Effects pages being turned, the odd cough (p5)
Effects map being flattened out (p5)

Effects footsteps. Door opening (p8)
Effects clatter of items lifted (p8)
Effects door bursting open (p9)
Effects door slam (p10)

Effects hum of freezer (p12)
Effects hum of voices. Tannoy (p14)

Effects wind. Distant barking of a dog (p17)
Effects rustling of jacket (p17)
Effects trickle of urine against wood (p17)
Effects urine trickles to a halt (p17)
Effects Brian struggling with Mark's zip (p18)

Effects glasses clattering. Low Russian voices (p20)
Effects louder pub sounds. Russian singing (p22)
Effects pub noises subside (p23)
Effects chair scrape as Brian stands (p23)
Effects the pub goes quiet (p23)
Effects tape switched off (p23)
Shostakovich/ "Symphony No 10 (under) (p23)
Effects wind buffeting canvas (p24)
Effects pub sounds (p25)
Effects gale blowing (p26)

Effects wind (p28)

Effects wind whistling past the open door (under) (p31)
Silence but for wind (p31)
Effects door slam. Crackling fire (under) (p31)
Fade (p31)
Effects crackling hearth (p32)
Effects hiss and stutter as log lands in flames (p32)

Effects plate and cutlery being placed on table (p32)

Effects scrape, then sound of ladder against brick (p35)
Effects Graham climbing ladder (p35)
Effects hammering (p36)
Effort distant hammering, rattling ladder (p37)
Effects wind (p38)
Effects click of camera shutter (p38)
Effects click of shutter (p38)
Effects crackling hearth, low Russian voices (p40)
Effects vodka glasses slammed on table (p40)
Effects glass on table (p40)
Effects crackling hearth (p41)
Effects wind blowing. Feet crunching on snow (p42)
Effects blowing wind, all else is silence (p42)
Effects click as tape cuts out (p44)
Effects noise of radio transmission and interference (p46)
Effects radio buzz (p46)
Effects transmission noise (p46)
Effects crackling hearth, low Russian voices (p48)
Effects wind buffeting canvas, frying sounds (p50)

Effects radio buzz (p52)
Effects buzz (p52)
Effects buzz (p52)
Effects paper being uncreased (p52)
Effects silence, but for the wind flapping the tent (p53)
Effects wind howls outside (p53)

Effects gale blowing (p54)
Effects wind blustering canvas (p55)
Effects howling gale (p56)

Effects wind (p57)
Effects wind blustering tent (p58)
Effects wind (p59)
Effects rustle of sleeping bag (p60)
Effects Mark crawling out of the sleeping bag (p60)
Effects zip being undone (p60)
Effects his feet on snow (p60)

Effects a squelch (p60)
Effects click as mic being switched off (p61)
Effects hiss of stove, frying (p62)
Effects an Elastoplast being unwrapped (p62)

Effects slight wind. Tent zip being undone (p64)
Effects slight squelch (p64)

Effects wind (p66)
Effects plastic being unwrapped (p66)
Effects Brian approaching in the snow (p66)
Effects plastic being wrapped away (p66)
Effects Brian collapsing on the snow (p66)

Effects wind buffeting canvas. Hiss of radio (p69)
Effects zip of tent opening (p69)
Effects zip of tent closing (p69)
Effects wind (p70)
Effects plastic being unwrapped (p70)
Effects plastic being scrumpled up and hidden (p70)
Effects hum of radio. Graham slurping tea (p72)

Effects wind (p76)
Effects gunshot. Footsteps in snow. Another gunshot (p76)
Silence but for wind (p76)
Effects wind buffeting canvas. Spoon against pan (p77)

Effects gale-force winds, very severe (p79)
Effects mic being buffeted, then shielded (p79)
Effects wind increasing (p79)
Effects bearhug, backs being slapped (p79)
Effects wind buffeting canvas (p80)

Effects gas stove burning, spoon against pan (p82)
Effects sleeping bag sounds (p82)
Effects plastic bag being scrumpled (p82)
Effects Brian moving (p82)
Effects Brian grabs plastic, unravelling it (p82)
Effects rummaging at plastic (p83)

Effects wind blustering canvas (p84)

Effects loud growling (p85)
Effects howling wind (p86)

Effects gunshot (p87)
Effects wind blustering canvas (p88)
Effects Brian grabs plastic, unravelling it (p89)
Effects a storm blowing outside (p90)
Effects cartridges being loaded (p90)
Effects gun being cocked (p91)
Effects gun being placed under bag (P91)
Effects radio buzz. Storm blowing (p92)
Effects interference (p92)

Effects deep, frightening rumbles under the ice (p94)
Effects ear-splitting cracking ice (p94)
Effects massive cracking ice (p94)
Effects tea being poured (p95)
Effects slurp of tea (p95)
Effects opening of a drawer, rummage of papers (p95)

Effects wind blustering tent (p98)
Effects zip being undone (p98)
Effects radio buzz (p100)
Effects click as radio is switched off (p100)

Effects wind (p102)
Effects wind (p102)

Effects wind buffeting canvas. Tea being drunk (p104)
Effects click of recorder being switched off (p104)

Effects wind (p106)

Effects wind (p108)

Effects wind. Canvas flapping (p110)
Effects growling bear outside of tent (p110)
Effects huge roaring sound (p110)
Effects panic sounds, scrambling around, looking for gun (p110)
Effects growls, very, very loud (p111)

Effects zip being opened. Furious growling for a moment, then fading into distance. Silence but for wind (p111)
Effects zip being undone (p112)
Effects wind buffeting canvas. Radio buzz (p113)

Effects radio buzz (p115)
Effects distort and transmission noise (p115)
Effects Brian trying to adjust frequency (p115)
Effects transmission whine (p115)
Effects distort (p115)
Effects Brian adjusting frequency (p115)
Effects transmission whine (p115)
Effects Mark switches off the radio (p115)
Effects click as tape recorder is switched off (p116)

Effects wind blustering across canvas (p117)

Effects howling wind (p119)

Effects wind (p120)
Effects transmission whine (p121)
Effects wind (p122)

Effects wind buffeting canvas (p123)
Effects wind (p124)
Effects radio buzz (p125)
Effects buzz (p125)
Effects buzz (p125)
Effects Graham talking biscuit out of packet (p125)
Effects interference (p125)
Effects buzz (p125)

Effects wind buffeting (p128)
Effects wind buffeting (p128)

Effects wind buffeting (p132)

Effects wind (p134)
Effects loud gunshot (p134)
Effects gunshot (p134)
Effects sound of gun being loaded (p134)

Effects gunshot (p134)
Effects sound of struggle ending in gunshot (p135)
Effects radio buzz (p136)
Effects Graham switching off radio (p136)
Effects radio interference (p137)
Effects long radio hiss (p137)
Effects long radio hiss (p137)
Effects wind (p138)
Effects zip of tent being opened (p138)

Effects cracking ice. Enormous splash (p140)
Effects splashing (p140)
Effects splashing (p140)
Effects mic being put on ground. Splashing (p140)
Effects splashing (p140)
Effects burning stove. Wind (p141)

Effects radio hiss (p142)
Effects interference (p142)
Effects buzz (p142)

Effects wind buffeting tent (p144)
Effects distant helicopter (p144)
Effects helicopter closer (p144)
Effects zip being opened (p144)
Effects gun being loaded (p144)
Effects helicopter above tent (p144)
Effects gunshot (p145)
Effects gunshot (p145)
Effects gunshots. Broken propeller sounds, followed by huge crash (p145)
Effects silence but the wind (p145)

Effects gale blowing (p146)

Effects splashing (p147)
Effects more splashing (p147)
Effects wind (p148)
Effects helicopter. A gunshot (p149)
Effects gunshots. Broken propeller sounds. Crash (p149)
Effects wind buffeting (p150)

Effects wind on tent (p151)
Effects click as tape is switched off (p151)

Effects radio crackle (p153)
Effects click as radio is switched off (p153
Effects gale outside (p155)
Effects zip opening (p155)
Effects zip closing behind him (p155)
Effects spoon against pan, beating eggs (p158)

Effects wind (p160)

Effects wind (p162)
Effects unpacking something from the sledge (p162)
Effects plastic being unwrapped. (p162)
Effects flag flapping in the breeze (p163)
Face (p163)
Effects can being opened. Low murmur of voices (p164)
Effects radio distort (p164)
Effects champagne cork being popped (p164)
Effects hiss (p165)
Effects wind (p166)
Effects shutter click (p166)
Effects paper being unwrapped (p166)
Effects click of shutter (p166)
Drunken scuffle (p168)
Effects click as mic is switched off (p168)
Effects wind (p170)
Silence but for wind (p170)
Effects wind picking up (p170)

THIS
IS
NOT
THE
END

Lightning Source UK Ltd.
Milton Keynes UK
UKOW01f1652260717
306107UK00001B/21/P